a gift to

Celeste Bounds

from

Alvia Torres

A Helen Exley Giftbook produced under license for Hallmark Cards, Inc.

Published simultaneously in 1992 by Exley Giftbooks in the USA and Exley Publications Ltd in Great Britain. This edition published by Exley Publications Ltd in Great Britain and supplied to Hallmark under license. All rights reserved. No part of this publication may be reproduced or transmitted in any form or by any means, electronic or mechanical, including photocopy, recording or any information storage and retrieval system without permission in writing from the Publisher.
Copyright © Helen Exley 1992
The moral right of the author has been asserted.
12 11 10
Edited and pictures selected by Helen Exley.
Typeset by Delta, Watford.
Printed in China.

**Exley Publications Ltd, 16 Chalk Hill, Watford,
Herts WD19 4BG, United Kingdom.
Exley Publications LLC, 232 Madison Avenue, Suite 1409,
New York, NY 10016, USA.**

www.Hallmark.com

Picture Credits: Exley Publications is very grateful to the following organizations for permission to reproduce their pictures: AKG, Bridgeman Art Library, Mary Evans, Explorer, Peter Kettle, Scala. Cover, title-page and endpapers © 2001 Hallmark Gift Books. Acknowledgements: The publishers would like to thank the following for permission to reprint copyright material. They would be pleased to hear from any copyright holders not here acknowledged. Roger Caras, extracts from A Celebration of Cats © 1986 Roger Caras, reprinted by permission of Robson Books Ltd and Simon & Schuster, Inc.; Eleanor Farjeon, "Cats" published by Oxford University Press, reprinted by permission of David Higham Associates Ltd; Paul Gallico, extracts from Honourable Cat, © 1972 Paul Gallico and Mathemata Anstalt, reprinted by permission of Souvenir Press Ltd and Crown Publishers Inc.; Ted Hughes, extract from "Esther's Tom Cat" from Lupercal, reprinted by permission of Faber & Faber Ltd; Doris Lessing, extracts from Particularly Cats and More Cats, published by Michael Joseph, copyright © Doris Lessing Productions Ltd, 1967, 1989, reprinted by permission of Penguin Books Ltd; Rod McKuen, "Me and the Cat", from Listen to the Warm by Rod McKuen. Copyright © 1967 by Rod McKuen, reprinted by permission of Random House, Inc.; Isha Mellor, extract from The Purr-fect Cat Book, reprinted by permission of the publisher, Piatkus Books Ltd; Rosalie Moore, extract from "Catalogue", reprinted by permission; © 1940, 1968 The New Yorker Magazine Inc.; Beatrix Potter, extract from The Journal of Beatrix Potter 1881-1897, transcribed by Leslie Linder, copyright © Frederick Warne & Co. 1966, 1989, reprinted by permission of Frederick Warne; Ian Serraillier, extract from "Miss Tibbles", reprinted by permission of the author.

cat

quotations

GIFT BOOKS

Selected for Hallmark by Helen Exley

EXLEY

WHAT LIFE IS ALL ABOUT

Often, when I have been feeling lonely, when a book has been thrust aside in boredom . . . I have lain back and stared at the shadows on the ceiling, wondering what life is all about . . . and then, suddenly, there is the echo of the swinging door, and across the carpet, walking with the utmost delicacy and precision, stalks "Four" or "Five" or Oscar. He sits down on the floor beside me, regarding my long legs, my old jumper, and my floppy arms, with a purely practical interest. Which part of this large male body will form the most appropriate lap? Usually he settles for the chest. Whereupon he springs up and there is a feeling of cold fur . . . and the tip of an icy nose, thrust against my wrist and a positive tattoo of purrs. And I no longer wonder what life is all about.

BEVERLEY NICHOLS

HONOURABLE CAT

I am Cat.
I am honourable.
I have pride.
I have dignity.
And I have memory.
For I am older than you.
I am older than your Gods; the Tree Gods,
the Stone Gods,
The thunder and Lightning and the Sun
Gods
And your God of Love
I too can love
But with only half a heart
And that I offer you.
Accept what I am able to give
For were I to give you all
I could not bear your inevitable treachery.
Let us remain honourable friends.

PAUL GALLICO (1896-1976)
FROM "HONOURABLE CAT"

ON KITTENS

A kitten is the delight of a household.
All day long a comedy is played out by an
incomparable actor.

CHAMPFLEURY (1821-1899)

The kitten was six weeks old. It was
enchanting, a delicate fairy-tale cat, whose
Siamese genes showed in the shape of the
face, ears, tail, and the subtle lines of its
body. . . . From the front, sitting with her
slender paws straight, she was an exotically
beautiful beast. She sat, a tiny thing, in the
middle of a yellow carpet, surrounded by
five worshippers, not at all afraid of us.
Then she stalked around that floor of the
house, inspecting every inch of it, climbed
up on to my bed, crept under the fold of a
sheet, and was at home.

DORIS LESSING, b. 1919

SHEER BEAUTY

A cat is beautiful at a distance - near-to he is
an inexhaustible matter for wonder: the
patterning of his eyes, the elaborations
of his ears, the beautiful precision of his
nostrils, the elaborate whorls of his face fur,
the elegance of his bones, the delicacy of his
sinews, the efficiency of his paws, the separate
aliveness of his tail. His mouth is incredibly
clean, incredibly pink.
His teeth are precision made. The roof is
rippled, his tongue rasped.
Everything he does is a perfection.

PAM BROWN, b.1928

Oh cat: I'd say, or pray: be-ooootiful cat!
Delicious cat! Exquisite cat! Satiny cat!
Cat like a soft owl, cat with paws like moths,
jewelled cat, miraculous cat!
Cat, cat, cat, cat.

DORIS LESSING, b. 1919

The flowers
think they are more
beautiful than we,
But they are wrong.

PAUL GALLICO

The smallest feline
is a masterpiece.

LEONARDO DA VINCI

MEMORIES OF CALVIN

$\mathcal{W}$e understood each other perfectly, but we never made any fuss about it; when I spoke his name and snapped my fingers, he came to me; when I returned home at night, he was pretty sure to be waiting for me near the gate, and would rise and saunter along the walk, as if his being there was purely accidental - so shy was he commonly of showing feeling. There was one thing he never did - he never rushed through an open doorway.

He never forgot his dignity. If he had asked to have the door opened; and was eager to go out, he always went out deliberately; I can see him now, standing on the sill, looking about at the sky as if he was thinking whether it was worthwhile to take an umbrella, until he was near having his tail shut in.

CHARLES DUDLEY WARNER
(1898-1976)

THE GARDENER'S CAT

The gardener's cat's called Mignonette,
She hates the cold, she hates the wet,
She sits among the hothouse flowers
And sleeps for hours and hours and hours.

She dreams she is a tiger fierce
With great majestic claws that pierce,
She sits by the hot-water pipes
And dreams about a coat of stripes;

And in her slumbers she will go
And stalks the sullen buffalo,
And then he roars across the brake
She does not wink, she does not wake.

It must be perfectly immense
To dream with such magnificence,
And pass the most inclement day
In this indeed stupendous way.

She dreams of India's sunny clime,
And only wakes at dinnertime,
And even then she does not stir
But waits till milk is brought to her.

How nice to be the gardener's cat,
She troubles not for mouse or rat,
But, when it's coming down in streams,
She sits among the flowers and dreams.

The gardener's cat would be the thing,
Her dreams are so encouraging;
She dreams that she's a tiger, yet
She's just a cat called Mignonette!

PATRICK R. CHALMERS

CONFESSION

I've been named Poosie, and
I am spoiled
Thoroughly, thoroughly spoiled, and I like it.
And don't let anyone tell you different.
I lie upon the softest cushions,
Under the downiest covers
And love every moment.
I get the cream off the top of the milk every day
And special double thick, heavy on Sundays,
And I lap it up.
My owner is besotted.
She hugs and kisses me
And carries me around with her all day,
And talks to me and I enjoy it.
I'm spoiled rotten, and, friends,
That's the life.
Whatever I want, I cry for,
Crab, lobster, caviare, fish roes, sardines, fillet,
white meat of chicken,
You name it, she's got it,
I get it.
I don't want to work, or hunt.

If ten snow-white mice were to saunter past
my nose,
I wouldn't lift a paw.
I'm greedy, graceless, shameless, lazy,
And luxury loving.
Everything that comes my way I take,
And yell for more.
I'm spoiled useless.
I admit it.
And I adore it.

PAUL GALLICO
(1896-1976)

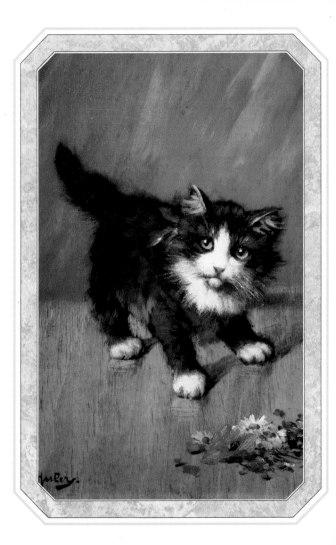

KITTEN VERSES

$\mathcal{A}$ kitten with a length of string
Is such a pretty, playful thing.
A kitten with a leaf to chase
Exhibits beauty, form and grace.
But I love kittens curled up, wise,
With ancient mystery in their eyes.

SALVATORE MARSIGLIA

I wish she wouldn't ask me if
I love the kitten more than her.
Of course I love her -
But I love the kitten too, And it has fur. . .

ANON

I like little Pussy, her coat is so warm,
And if I don't hurt her,
she'll do me no harm.
So I'll not pull her tail, nor drive her away,
But Pussy and I very gently will play.

SOURCE UNKNOWN, c.1843

CAT ON THE HEARTH

The firelight flickers on the Chinese tray
And on the books set snugly in their rack;
Copper and silver flow beneath its play,
The chairs are placed - what is it that
we lack?

She comes. With each foot delicately placed,
Advancing like a vestal to the rite,
She scorns to move with unbecoming haste
Or note the lesser objects in her sight.

She settles couchant; curves one placid paw
Beneath her chest; now curves its mate
the same;
Yields to the promptings of some ancient law
And fastens thoughtful eyes upon the flame.

Now let the night wind rise, the grey
storm come.
The cat is on the hearth - we are at home.

SILENCE BUCK BELLOWS

WHO OWNS WHO?

*I'd like to think I owned the cat
That condescends to share my flat;
I give him of my rationed food
And cater to his every mood.
I'd like to think he'd go to seed
If I weren't there to meet his need,
And yet the fact is plain to see -
The pesky, doggone cat owns me!*

RUTH M. OUTWATER

*Dogs will play football, walk a tightrope,
and do backflips; bears will roller-skate
or ride seesaws, and seals render "My
Country 'Tis of Thee" on a bank of tooters,
but your pet cat won't even come when
you call it if it doesn't feel like it or doesn't
think there might be something in it
for itself.*

PAUL GALLICO (1896-1976)

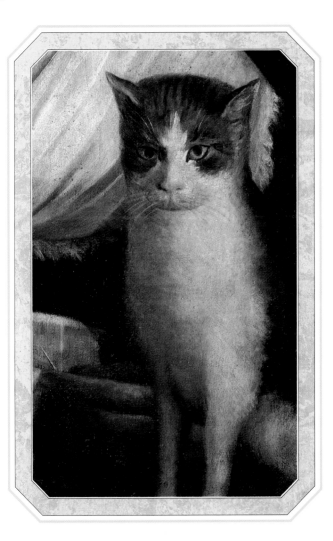

WHAT IS A CAT?

The house-cat is a four-legged
quadruped, the legs as usual being at
the corners. It is what is sometimes
called a tame animal, though it feeds on
mice and birds of prey. Its colours are
striped, it does not bark, but breathes
through its nose instead of its mouth.
Cats also mow, which you all have
heard. Cats have nine liveses, but which
is seldom wanted in this country, coz'
of Christianity. Cats eat meat and most
anythink speshuelly where you can't
afford. That is all about cats.

A SCHOOLBOY'S ESSAY, 1903

ANOTHER WORLD

He shut his eyes while Saha (the cat)
kept vigil, watching all the invisible signs
that hover over sleeping human beings
when the light is out.

FROM *"THE CAT"*, 1933

A cat's eyes are windows enabling us to see
into another world.

IRISH LEGEND

Lift up your large black satin eyes which
are like cushions where one sinks! Fawn at
my feet, fantastic Sphinx! and sing me all
your memories!

OSCAR WILDE (1856-1900)

Daylong this tomcat lies stretched flat
As an old rough mat, no mouth and no eyes.
Continual wars and wives are what
Have tattered his ears and battered his head.

Like a bundle of old rope and iron
Sleeps till blue dusk. Then reappear
His eyes, green as ringstones: he yawns
wide red,
Fangs fine as a lady's needle and bright.

. . . He leaps and lightly
Walks upon sleep, his mind on the moon.
Nightly over the round world of men,
Over the roofs go his eyes and outcry.

TED HUGHES, b. 1930
"ESTHER'S TOMCAT"

BEWARE OF THE CAT

We tie bright ribbons around their necks, and occasionally little tinkling bells, and we affect to think that they are as sweet and vapid as the coy name "kitty" by which we call them would imply. It is a curious illusion. For, purring beside our fireplaces and pattering along our back fences, we have got a wild beast as uncowed and uncorrupted as any under heaven.

ALAN DEVOE

When I grow up I mean to be
A Lion large and fierce to see.
I'll mew so loud that Cook in fright
Will give me all the cream in sight.
And anyone who dares to say
"Poor Puss" to me will rue the day.
Then having swallowed him I'll creep
Into the Guest Room Bed to sleep.

OLIVER HERFORD (AFTER R.L.S.)

The last thing I would accuse a cat
of is innocence.

EDWARD PALEY (1786-1847)

When a cat is offended every square
centimetre of him is offended. Men and
women of power and intellect have been
brought to their knees by cats who have
turned their backs on them.

A. P. REILLY

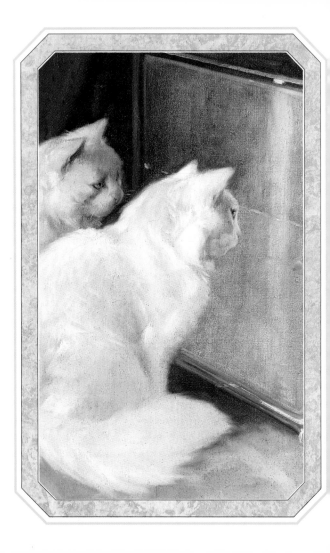

INSTINCT

"*Japanese goldfish,*
With your gossamer tail,
You are the loveliest creature
I have ever seen."

"*Japanese kitten,*
Put your tongue back in where it belongs
And go away.
I know exactly what you are thinking."

PAUL GALLICO (1896-1976)

Sunday, January 27 1884 - There was
another story in the paper a week or so
since. A gentleman had a favourite cat
whom he taught to sit at the dinner table
where it behaved very well. He was in the
habit of putting any scraps he left on to the
cat's plate. One day puss did not take his
place punctually, but presently appeared
with two mice, one of which it placed on
its master's plate, the other on its own.

BEATRIX POTTER (1866-1943)

THE CAT AND THE MOON

The cat went here and there
And the moon spun round like a top
And the nearest kin of the moon,
The creeping cat, looked up.
Black Minnaloushe stared at the moon,
For, wander and wail as he would,
The pure cold light in the sky
Troubled his animal blood.
Minnaloushe runs in the grass
Lifting his delicate feet.
Do you dance, Minnaloushe, do you dance?
When two close kindred meet,
What better than call a dance?
Maybe the moon may learn,
Tired of that courtly fashion
A new dance turn.

Minnaloushe creeps through the grass
From moonlit place to place,
The sacred moon overhead
has taken a new phase.
Does Minnaloushe know that his pupils
Will pass from change to change,
And that from round to crescent,
From crescent to round they range?
Minnaloushe creeps through the grass
Alone, important and wise,
And lifts to the changing moon
his changing eyes.

W. B. YEATS (1865-1939)

OFF TO SLEEP...

When I am cosied into sleep
my cat demands the door,
but when at last I'm warm again
he hammers on the window pane
- and I am up once more,
open the casement, see him leap,
Nijinsky, from the ledge;
a ghost of leaves and night and rain
he settles on the counterpane;
and I am left the edge.

PAM BROWN, b.1928

In the morning, when she wishes me to
wake, she crouches on my chest, and pats
my face with her paw. Or, if I am on my
side, she crouches looking into my face.
Soft, soft touches of her paw. I open my
eyes, say I don't want to wake. I close my
eyes. Cat gently pats my eyelids. Cat licks

my nose. Cat starts purring, two inches from my face. Cat, then, as I lie pretending to be asleep, delicately bites my nose. I laugh and sit up. At which she bounds off my bed and streaks downstairs - to have the back door opened if it is winter, to be fed, if it is summer.

DORIS LESSING, b. 1919

CATS SLEEP ANYWHERE

CATS SLEEP
ANYWHERE,
ANY TABLE
ANY CHAIR,
TOP OF PIANO,
WINDOW-LEDGE,
IN THE MIDDLE,
ON THE EDGE,
OPEN DRAWER,
EMPTY SHOE,
ANYBODY'S
LAP WILL DO,
FITTED IN A
CARDBOARD BOX,
IN THE CUPBOARD
WITH YOUR FROCKS -
ANYWHERE!
THEY DON'T CARE!
CATS SLEEP
ANYWHERE.

ELEANOR FARJEON (1881-1965)

Cat's cradle,
Cat's slumber,
Soft slumber;
Sleep softly
All cats....

PAUL GALLICO (1896-1976)
EXTRACT FROM *"SLEEP"*

SURRENDER

Let others praise the cat
And rhapsodize
About her velvet tread
And amber eyes.
I never liked the feline.
Yet, this first cool Fall day,
Before the furnace started,
I looked out upon my door-stoop
And espied a long gray cat.
Her sinuous back was curled
Around a straying sunbeam
Which seemed to catch and hold her
In a deep and friendly dream.
The sight brought warm comfort
To my lonely flat ...
Which is a bit more cheerful ...
Now, that I have a cat.

EVELYN HICKMAN

CAT AND DOG COMPARED

The dog is a hearty beast; you can ruffle his coat, and slap him on the back, and he'll beam at you. The fastidious cat hates to have his fur mussed, and loathes any show of heartiness. You must approach him quite differently. Ceremonial is required. A man who loved and owned dogs, but had never kept a cat, once went up to my mother's Pinkle Purr, and saying "Hello, old chap! You magnificent fellow!" gave her beloved tyrant a friendly smack on the behind. A dog would have contorted with delight. Pinkle Purr gave the visitor one mighty scratch, and fled in horror, his majesty outraged. It was as though a Cockney had bawled "Wot cher, Cock!" in the Throne Room.

KATHARINE L. SIMMS

Dogs live with you, cats board with you.

PAM BROWN, b. 1928

Humans have remade dogs to suit their own ends. Cats are exactly the same as they were ten thousand years ago.

MARION C. GARRETTY, b. 1917

TAFFY TOPAZ

Taffy, the topaz-coloured cat,
Thinks now of this and now of that,
But chiefly of his meals.
Asparagus, and cream, and fish,
Are objects of his Freudian wish;
What you don't give, he steals.

His gallant heart is strongly stirred
By clink of plate or flight of bird,
He has a plumy tail;
At night he treads on stealthy pad
As merry as Sir Galahad
A-seeking of the Grail.

His amiable amber eyes
Are very friendly, very wise;
Like Buddha, grave and fat,
He sits, regardless of applause,
And thinking, as he kneads his paws,
What fun to be a cat!

CHRISTOPHER MORLEY

Hearths are quite the favourite place
For cats to slip into good grace:
They stretch where flames high-light
their fur,
Tuning the room with soothing purr.
At charming they are extra smart,
Knowing sly wiles to win one's heart.

Undoubtedly the prudent cat
Is nature's choicest diplomat.

LEE RICHARD HAYMAN

LORDLY FRIEND

Stately, kindly, lordly friend
Condescend
Here to sit by me and turn
Glorious eyes that smile and burn,
Golden eyes, love's lustrous meed,
On the golden page I read.

ALGERNON CHARLES SWINBURNE
(1837-1909)

*A cat is only technically an animal,
being divine.*

ROBERT LYND (1879-1949)

*Cats, as a class, have never completely
got over the snootiness caused by the fact
that in ancient Egypt they were
worshipped as gods.*

P. G. WODEHOUSE (1881-1975)

*In Egypt: Under no conditions, under threat of
death could anyone kill a cat. People were
executed for even killing a cat accidentally.
And when a cat died, the whole family,
and probably their closest friends, went
into mourning, the measure of their
personal loss signalled by their shaving off
their eyebrows.*

ROGER A. CARAS

PURR . . .

*... Sometimes I like her calm, unwild,
gentle as a sleeping child,*

*and wonder as she lies, a fur ring,
curled upon my lap, unstirring -
is it me or Tibbles purring?*

IAN SERRAILLIER
EXTRACT FROM *"MISS TIBBLES"*

Cats make one of the most satisfying
sounds in the world: they purr. Almost all
cats make us feel good about ourselves
because they let us know they feel good
about us, about themselves, and about our
relationship with them. A purring cat is a
form of high praise, like a gold star on a
test paper. It is reinforcement of something
we would all like to believe about ourselves
- that we are nice.

ROGER CARAS

A LIFE OF LUXURY

Tsar Nicholas I of Russia fed his cat, Vashka, a celebratory concoction of the best caviare poached in rich champagne, with finely minced French dormouse, unsalted butter, cream, whipped woodcock's egg and hare's blood. Rather than trouble his servants, Doctor Johnson himself purchased oysters for his cat, Hodge.

DAVID TAYLOR

A cat knows how to be comfortable, how to get the people around it to serve it. In a tranquil domestic situation, the cat is a veritable manipulative genius. It seeks the soft, it seeks the warm, it prefers the quiet and it loves to be full. It displays, when it gets its own way in these matters, a degree of contentment we would all like to emulate.

ROGER CARAS

THE SURE-FOOTED CAT

Cats sleep fat and walk thin.
Cats, when they sleep, slump;
When they wake, stretch and begin
Over, pulling their ribs in.
Cats walk thin.

ROSALIE MOORE,
FROM "CATALOGUE"

Cats, no less liquid than their shadows,
Offer no angles to the wind.
They slip, diminished, neat, through
loopholes
Less than themselves.

A.S.J. TESSIMOND
(1902-1962)

Her ears, lightly fringed with white that looked silver, lifted and moved, back, forward, listening and sensing. Her face turned, slightly, after each new sensation, alert. Her tail moved, in another dimension, as if its tip was catching messages her other organs could not. She sat poised, air-light, looking, hearing, feeling, smelling, breathing, with all of her, fur, whiskers, ears - everything, in delicate vibration.

DORIS LESSING, b.1919

If a fish is the movement of water embodied, given shape, then cat is a diagram and pattern of subtle air.

DORIS LESSING, b.1919

Chinese parents used to embroider a cat's head on the shoes of a baby learning to walk, to make it surefooted.

ISHA MELLOR

DREAMING

The greater cats with golden eyes
Stare out between the bars.
Deserts are there, and different skies,
And night with different stars.

VITA SACKVILLE-WEST (1892-1962)

When Tabby crouches by the fire,
Primly agaze, her eyes are rings
Of agate flame: and strange desire
Burns there, and old unholy things.

Surges on dream the lost Delight:
And off she goes, careering down
the windy archways of the night,
Afar on flying broomsticks blown.

R.W.D. FULLER

THE CAT WHO WALKS
BY HIMSELF

Cat: a pygmy lion who
loves mice, hates dogs, and
patronizes human beings.

OLIVER HERFORD

It is a difficult matter to gain the
affection of a cat. He is a philosophical,
methodical animal, tenacious of his
own habits, fond of order and neatness,
and disinclined to extravagant
sentiment. He will be your friend, if he
finds you worthy of friendship, but not
your slave.

THEOPHILE GAUTIER (1811-1872)

Cat said, "I am not a friend, and I am not a
servant. I am the Cat who walks by himself,
and I wish to come into your Cave."

RUDYARD KIPLING (1865-1936)

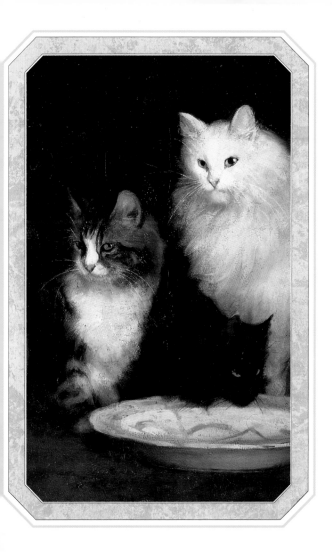

A COMFORT TO US

Hear our prayer, Lord, for all animals,
May they be well-fed and well-treated
and happy:
Protect them from hunger and fear and
suffering:
And, we pray, protect specially, dear Lord,
The little Cat who is the companion of our
home,
Keep her safe as she goes abroad,
And bring her back to comfort us.

AN OLD RUSSIAN PRAYER

Demanding - true; but also he
Deliberately sets out to be
A comfort in adversity.

GEORGE PARKER

One small cat changes coming home to an
empty house to coming home.

PAM BROWN

Once it has given its love, what absolute confidence, what fidelity of affection! It will make itself the companion of your hours of work, of loneliness, or of sadness. It will lie the whole evening on your knee, purring and happy in your society, and leaving the company of creatures of its own society to be with you.

THEOPHILE GAUTIER

ME AND THE CAT

We've seen so many winters come
and watched so many old years go
and held so many hands at dawn
we never really got to know.
Lying down someplace shady and flat,
me in my shirttails, him with his
whiskersme and the cat.

We've done so many foolish things
and yet the days have served us well.
We've given all our smiles away
when there were some we cared to sell.
Livin' the good life without gettin' fat,
me in my shirttails, him with his
whiskersme and the cat.

Looking back few friends had we
but I've got him and he's got me.
And when the golden minute comes

when we no longer wake to smell
the river where the wild swans sailed
the orchard where the blossoms fell,
we'll smile a little thinkin' of that.
Me in my shirt-tails, him with his
whiskers
me and the cat.

ROD MCKUEN